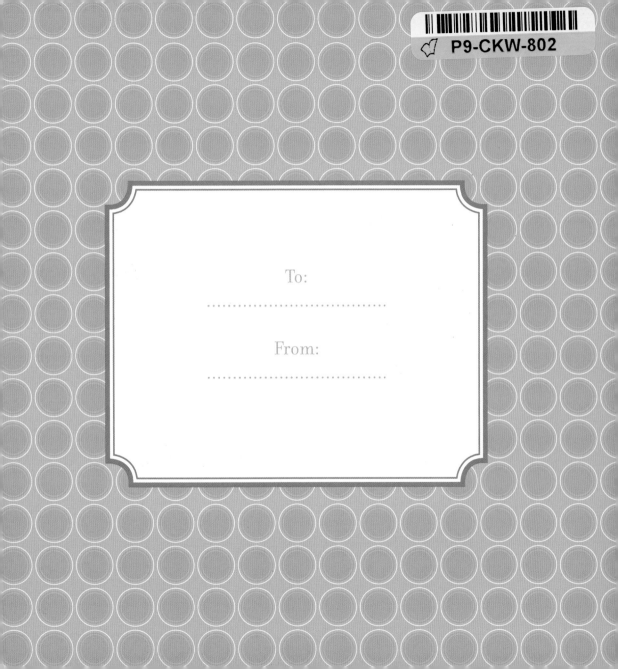

To:

....

From:

....

Other books in this series

Mother's Love

Love You, Dad

True Love

Friends Forever

The World Awaits

The Little Book of Thanks

Amazing Moms

the wisdom *of* moms

Love and Lessons From the Animal Kingdom

Bridget E. Hamilton

NATIONAL GEOGRAPHIC

Washington, D.C.

Since 1888, the National Geographic Society has funded more than 12,000 research, exploration, and preservation projects around the world. National Geographic Partners distributes a portion of the funds it receives from your purchase to National Geographic Society to support programs including the conservation of animals and their habitats.

National Geographic Partners
1145 17th Street NW
Washington, DC 20036-4688 USA

Become a member of National Geographic and activate
your benefits today at natgeo.com/jointoday.

For information about special discounts for bulk purchases, please contact
National Geographic Books Special Sales: specialsales@natgeo.com

For rights or permissions inquiries, please contact National Geographic
Books Subsidiary Rights: bookrights@natgeo.com

ISBN: 978-1-4262-1817-0

Printed in Hong Kong

16/THK/1

To my mom, thank you for sharing
your wisdom and kindness

introduction

Moms can be feathered or furry, they can live in the mountains, at the water's edge, or in the desert. They make homes out of mud and sticks and in caves. They might care for a whole litter of newborns or just have a little one to watch over. There are a number of things that make moms unique, but there is always one thing that they have in common: love. Sharing their love is just one of the many things that moms do for us. They also teach us compassion, encourage our dreams, and dedicate themselves to our well-being. On the following pages you'll learn the many ways animal moms show love for their babies and how their wisdom inspires us all.

It is a myth that a mother rabbit will abandon her babies if they are touched by a human. Mom will do anything to reunite her family.

True wisdom lies in gathering the precious things out of each hour as it goes by.

E.S. BOUTON

Grizzly bears are territorial and view even young cubs as a threat.
The mama bear must be willing to fight for the survival of her children.

At swimming time, elephant calves will splash and blow bubbles while their mother sprinkles them with water from her trunk.

The family is one of
nature's masterpieces.

GEORGE SANTAYANA

grit

The mountainous terrain of Central Asia is a harsh, cold place, but for snow leopards this is an ideal location to live and for a mom to raise her young. A mom-to-be finds a secluded shelter in the rocky environment, preparing a den from her soft underbelly fur so that she can welcome her litter of cubs and nurse them in hiding for the first few months. Mom knows that soon the cubs will have to develop the grit needed to survive in this rugged landscape, and they begin accompanying her out of the den around three months of age. The cubs stumble along in mom's footsteps until they too master the snow leopard's innate ability to navigate the mountains with grace. She keeps them close for the first year or so, serving as the singular provider and protector before they go out on their own.

Snow leopards are reclusive big cats, sometimes called "mountain ghosts" by locals because of their secretive nature.

Start by doing what's necessary,
then what's possible, and
**suddenly you are doing
the impossible.**

ST. FRANCIS OF ASSISI

*Flamingos are born white, then turn gray, and won't get pink plumage
until they are one to three years old.*

The simple things are also
the most extraordinary things,
and only the wise can see them.

PAULO COELHO

*Mother hedgehogs teach their babies to forage for food
and to roll into a prickly ball for protection.*

affection

A newborn gorilla need not look further than her mother to receive a comforting, affectionate touch. For the first five months of life she is in almost constant contact with her mother, clinging to her fur. This connection helps develop a very strong bond and keeps the vulnerable baby safe. The close relationship continues for the first few years as the baby grows, traveling on her mother's back. She learns from her mother and nurses for up to three years, all the while sleeping close to her at night in their shared nest. The baby gorilla will develop quickly, walking in the first six months, but she never wanders far from her mother—her source of affection and safety. As the baby reaches three years of age, she will become more independent and begin exploring with the other youngsters in the group, but the tender bond formed between mother and child endures.

Unlike their powerful parents, newborn gorillas are tiny—weighing only 4 pounds (1.8 kg).

The soul is healed by being with children.

FYODOR DOSTOYEVSKY

A domestic puppy, such as the English bulldog, becomes a well-socialized pet by watching its mother interact with humans.

Mother is **the home we come from.** She is nature, soil, ocean.

ERICH FROMM

Alligators carry their babies on their heads or inside their mouths.

creativity

What more beautiful place is there to raise your young than along the coastlines of North America? The location might be nice, but for the Least Tern, the task of caring for newly hatched chicks is no day at the beach. With a nest located right along the water's edge a mother bird has to be creative in her approach to keeping her hatchlings safe and sound. Using her body like a parasol, the mother tern stands over the nest, shading her chicks from the sun's rays. When the temperatures begin to rise, mom may go for a dip, allowing her to delicately cool her chicks with her wet belly feathers. This creative solution to keeping everyone comfortable is also a risk. Getting wet makes her more odorous, potentially attracting predators, but it is a risk she is willing to take for her brood.

Least Terns form colonies that can range from five to 200 pairs.

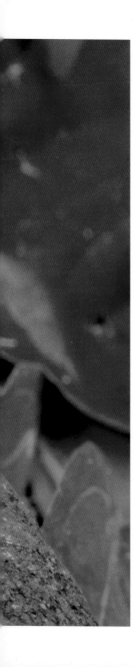

Being deeply loved by
someone gives you strength,
while **loving someone deeply**
gives you courage.

LAO-TZU

Adult blue poison dart frogs grow to only about 2 inches (5 cm) in length.

There is no way to be **a perfect mother,** and a million ways to be a good one.

JILL CHURCHILL

Female sea otters are among nature's hardest working and most attentive moms.
A pup rides on its mother's chest until it is about two months old.

guidance

Meerkats are known for their strong family groups, where each member has a role and pitching in to help each other is commonplace. Learning how to navigate life in the extreme environments of southern Africa, where desert temperatures can reach 100°F (37.8°C), is not an easy task for the family's young pups. Pups rely on older meerkats to teach them how to handle their often dangerous prey, such as scorpions, reptiles, and insects. Responding to the pups' cries for food, older meerkats will deliver prey that they've either killed or disabled so that it's safe for the young ones to eat. The meerkats introduce the pups to live prey as they get older and gain more confidence in handling their food.

Raising meerkat pups is a family affair, with mom, dad, and siblings all teaching them how to play and forage.

We can only be said to be alive in those moments when our hearts are **conscious of our treasures.**

THORNTON WILDER

A fawn and its mother will separate while she goes to feed,
but her baby's distress call will bring her running.

Only love can be **divided endlessly** and still not diminish.

ANNE MORROW LINDBERGH

*There is some evidence that a hen begins to vocalize
to her chicks the day before they hatch.*

compassion

At first glance, a lumbering elephant seal does not seem like a compassionate, loving animal. But looks can be deceiving! Elephant seal rookeries are crowded with mothers and their babies, but once her pup is born, mom learns his scent and listens for his signature cry that she can identify among the commotion. If a pup does get lost there is a chance it will be adopted by another elephant seal cow. The foster mother will suckle the pup and raise him as her own. Newborn pups weigh about 75 pounds (34 kg), but soon gain weight and strength, reaching 300 pounds (136 kg) in the first month. With a hungry pup to feed, mom has been relying on her fat stores, dramatically losing weight as he gains. Soon she leaves to go feed, and her pup is left to head to the sea, his true home.

Southern elephant seals can dive more than 4,921 feet (1,500 m)
deep and remain submerged for up to two hours.

What is a family, after all, except memories?—**haphazard and precious** as the contents of a catchall drawer in the kitchen.

JOYCE CAROL OATES

Love is not a because,
it's a **no matter what.**

JODI PICOULT

Spotted hyenas live in large clans—up to 80 members—ruled by an alpha female.

resourcefulness

It doesn't matter where your home is, what matters is who you share it with. The Moupin pika has few options when it comes to shelter in the Himalaya and surrounding mountain ranges, so this resourceful pika digs its own high-elevation burrow. Mom also prepares caches of seeds and plants to feed on during the long winter months. Moupin pika families are most often made up of a mother, father, and siblings from multiple breeding seasons. These highly social mammals not only share space but they share a language of squeaks and vocal signals. In the early days of the new litter, a new sound is introduced— the warning call. An adult sounds the alarm when a predator is sighted, drawing perhaps lethal attention to itself while others move the babies to safety.

Moupin pikas help groom each other and bestow affection through nose rubbing and other forms of contact.

Where we love is home—home
that our feet may leave, but not
our hearts.

OLIVER WENDELL HOLMES, SR.

*While a young foal sleeps, a zebra mother or another adult will stay
awake to watch for predators.*

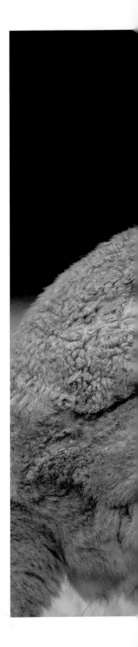

The best thing to hold onto
in life **is each other.**

AUDREY HEPBURN

A mother kangaroo and her joey may engage in hugging, kissing,
and grooming when reunited after a brief separation.

encouragement

Dolphin calves have a lot to live up to, especially when growing alongside a mom who can reach speeds greater than 18 miles an hour (29 kph). But a dolphin mom would never leave her calf behind; instead she encourages him to keep up by creating a slipstream as she swims. With her calf swimming just 4 to 12 inches (10 to 30 cm) behind her tail, mom creates an almost magnetic force by displacing the water around her as she swims, cocooning the calf in a calm wake that allows him to keep up with his fast-moving mom. Mom doesn't just tow her baby behind her to keep tabs on him—when a dolphin is first born he doesn't have enough blubber to stay afloat, so mom has to swim to keep him buoyant. She also knows a newborn needs plenty of rest and nutrition, and her slipstream allows the baby to get both. Thanks to the encouragement of his mom, the baby will soon be able to keep up with the adults of the pod.

A calf stays with its mother for three to five years. If they meet later in life, they will recognize each other as a dolphin they have met before.

If the only prayer you said was
thank you, that would be enough.

MEISTER ECKHART

*On the Serengeti, lionesses not only rear the cubs
but also do the majority of the hunting for the pride.*

When your life is on course with its purpose, you are at your most powerful. **And though you may stumble,** you will not fall.

OPRAH WINFREY

A foal and its mother form a strong bond in the first hour after birth as the baby learns to stand, nurse, and recognize its mother's nicker.

dedication

There is no truer saying than "busy as a beaver." These hard-working moms have between one and four kits in each litter, and mom needs to be prepared for their arrival. Beavers make their home in lodges, which are woven together from mud, sticks, and grasses and located on or very close to the water. Over time, beavers make improvements to increase the size of the lodge. Before the kits arrive, mom takes time to create a welcoming nursery within the lodge with a floor that is soft enough for her newborns. Kits begin swimming 24 hours after birth, setting off to explore their environment. Kits will learn from their parents for two years before getting busy building their own lodges, near their hardworking parents, of course.

Some extremely large beaver lodges may hold several families.

There was never **a child so lovely** but his mother was glad to get asleep.

RALPH WALDO EMERSON

When prey is scarce, a great gray owl will eat
the minimum amount to give more to her chicks.

We are biologically, cognitively, physically, and spiritually **wired to love,** be loved, and to belong.

BRENÉ BROWN

A mother humpback whale and her calf are inseparable for the first year.
They swim next to each other, often touching flippers.

loyalty

Having a loyal member of the family to rely on is a comfort that moms know not to take for granted. Capybaras have a loyal family base that can be relied on when it comes to raising pups. Found east of the Andes in Central and South America along the shoreline of rivers, ponds, and marshes, capybaras live in a community made up of approximately 10 members. When a newborn litter of capybaras arrive, the mom trusts the other females in her group to keep an eye on the youngsters and protect them from any threats. It takes them a little while before they are able to join the group, but once they are mobile they have many "moms" to comfort, protect, and care for them.

Capybaras take the prize for being the largest rodent in the world.

The more love you give away,
the more love you will have.

JOHN O'DONOHUE

Red hartebeest mothers seek out dry pastures
to camouflage their calves in the grass.

There are only two ways
to live your life. One is as
though nothing is a miracle.
The other is **as though
everything is a miracle.**

ALBERT EINSTEIN

*A koala joey lives in its mother's pouch for six months, then continues to cling
to her body for another year, either cradled to her chest or riding on her back.*

savvy

Anything with the word "giant" in its name might not seem like the savviest creature around, but the giant anteater of Central and South America is most certainly a savvy mom. Mom and baby stay together for close to two years, while the baby nurses for the first two months, and relies on her mom for extra protection through the first nine months. At the same time, mom needs to eat—she can consume almost 30,000 ants a day— and for the baby to stay close, she needs to climb on her mom's back. Mom knows the baby will be safe because she blends in with the stripes and bands of color on her mom's fur— the perfect camouflage. She is born with the same markings, making her a mini-version of her savvy mom.

Giant anteaters do not have teeth, but to capture prey
their tongue can extend up to 2 feet (0.6 m).

Love the moment, and the energy of that moment will spread beyond all boundaries.

SISTER CORITA KENT

Free-range farm pigs will make a nest for their families,
gathering extra straw for warmth when the piglets are young.

Life shrinks or expands in
proportion to **one's courage.**

ANAÏS NIN

White rhinos usually give birth to only one calf
every three to five years, making every child precious.

tenderness

When it comes to nesting, we know birds do it best. There is something special, though, about the tenderness a female prothonotary warbler shows in building her babies' home. After dad has picked out the best location, usually a low cavity in a tree near a pond or another slow-moving body of water, mom gets to work. Over the course of a few days the mom-to-be is busy preparing an ideal nest lined with soft grasses, feathers, and leaf stems. After the work is complete she will lay three to seven eggs per clutch and wait patiently for the chicks to hatch a couple weeks later. Mom, dad, and their chicks will make full use of the sweet home mom has built.

A flock of warblers is known as a bouquet.

I use the word *love,* not
meaning sentimentality, but
a condition so strong that it
may be that which holds the
stars in their heavenly positions.

MAYA ANGELOU

*American bison herds are made up of females and their calves. Young mothers
and their daughters form particularly close, long-lasting relationships.*

By three methods **we may learn wisdom:** first, by reflection, which is noblest; second, by imitation, which is easiest; and third by experience, which is the bitterest.

CONFUCIUS

An infant ring-tailed lemur will "purr" while it is groomed by its mother.

caring

Panda cubs have a lot to live up to. At birth a cub weighs only a few ounces and measures about as long as a stick of butter. When he is first born the cub is helpless—he has little fur and is blind. In addition to protection, the cub needs to be fed every two hours, and he'll let mom know with a cry for milk. When she is not busy feeding, mom will hold her cub gently until he is about three months old, the age when his eyes have opened and he starts to crawl. Over the next 15 months or so, mom continues to care for her cub as he follows her into the forest and eats his first bamboo. Pandas of all ages love to play, but cubs are particularly silly. Mom gets the all-important role of being a tireless playmate.

Adult pandas spend almost 12 hours a day eating bamboo.

What a difference it makes to
come home to a child!

MARGARET FULLER

A baby porcupine is called a pup or a porcupette.

Sometimes the **laughter in mothering** is the recognition of the ironies and absurdities. Sometimes, though, it's just pure, unthinking delight.

BARBARA SCHAPIRO

Baby baboons play by swinging from vines, chasing each other, and making toys out of found objects like feathers.

courage

It takes a lot of courage to stand up to an enemy, but for a moose cow looking out for her newborn, it comes naturally. Moose cows give birth to one or two calves each spring, and often find themselves needing to play protector as well as caretaker. Recently, a moose in Sweden was caught on camera courageously attempting to defend her young from two wolves that sneaked up on them. A moose is not only tall—standing anywhere from 4.5 feet to 6.9 feet (1.4 m to 2.1 m)—she is also limber and can wield her sharp, pointed hooves as a powerful defense mechanism. Moose mothers like to keep their calves close, until the calves reach about a year old, when they separate and the yearlings courageously go out on their own.

Moose are the second largest land animal in both North America and Europe.

Where there is love
there is life.

MAHATMA GANDHI

Cheetah cubs often fall prey to lions and hyenas, so their mother must move the den site every couple days, gently transporting one cub at a time in her mouth.

You will do foolish things,
but **do them with enthusiasm.**

COLETTE

*A mother Egyptian goose lines her nest
with soft, downy feathers to comfort her nestlings.*

illustration credits

A Soay sheep lamb will suckle its mother by instinct but must be taught to graze by observing its mother.

Cherish *the* Moms *and* Dads *in* Your Life *with* These Heartfelt Celebrations *of* Parenthood

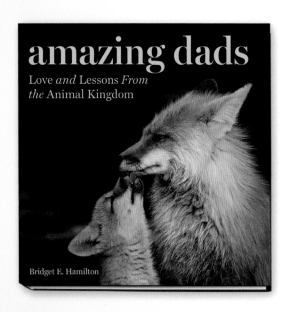

amazing dads

Love *and* Lessons *From the* Animal Kingdom

Bridget E. Hamilton

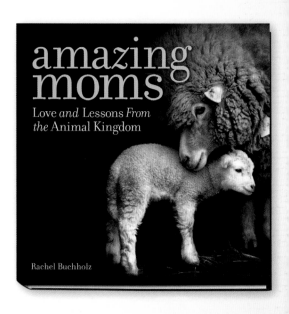

amazing moms

Love *and* Lessons *From the* Animal Kingdom

Rachel Buchholz